@Copyright 2020by Alicia Reed- All rights reserved.

This document is geared towards providing exact and reliable information in regards to the topic and issue covered. The publication is sold with the idea that the publisher is not required to render accounting, officially permitted, or otherwise, qualified services. If advice is necessary, legal or professional, a practiced individual in the profession should be ordered.

Under no circumstance will any legal responsibility or blame be held against the publisher for any reparation, damages, or monetary loss due to the information herein, either directly or indirectly.

Legal Notice:

The book is copyright protected. This is only for personal use. You cannot amend, distribute, sell, use, quote or paraphrase any part or the content within this book without the consent of the author.

Disclaimer Notice:

Please note the information contained within this document is for educational and entertainment purposes only. Every attempt has been made to provide accurate, up to date and reliable complete information.

No warranties of any kind are expressed or implied. Readers acknowledge that the author is not engaging in the rendering of legal, financial, medical or professional advice. The content of this book has been derived from various sources. Please consult a licensed professional before attempting any techniques outlined in this book.

CONTENTS

INSTANT OMNI AIR FRYER TOASTER OVEN OVERVIEW 6
    Cooking Timetable 6
    Cooking with the Omni Toaster Oven 8
    Cooking Tips 10
    Smart Programs 11
    Care and Cleaning 13

Breakfast Recipes 14
    Crispy Potato Rosti 14
    Toasties and Sausage in Egg Pond 15
    Banana Bread 15
    Peanut Butter Banana Bread 16
    Flavorful Bacon Cups 17
    Stylish Ham Omelet 18
    Aromatic Potato Hash 18
    Healthy Tofu Omelet 19
    Spinach Muffins 20
    Chicken Omelet 21
    Tofu & Mushroom Omelet 22
    Bacon, Kale & Tomato Frittata 23
    Tomato Quiche 24

Poultry Recipes 25
    Simple Roasted Chicken 25
    Marinated Chicken Legs 26
    Spicy Chicken Thighs 27
    Crispy Chicken Drumsticks 28
    Sweet & Spicy Chicken Drumsticks 29
    Crispy Chicken Breast 30
    Buttered Turkey Wings 31
    Rosemary Turkey Breast 32
    Greek Chicken Thighs 33
    Baked Dill Feta Chicken 34
    Lemon Garlic Chicken 35
    Delicious Chicken Tenders 36
    Herb Chicken Thighs 37
    Easy Chili Garlic Chicken Wings 38

  Chicken Casserole 39
Meat Recipes 40
  Provencal Pork 40
  Lamb with Brussels Sprouts 41
  Zesty Pork Skewers 42
  Beef Strips with Vegetables 43
  Pork Garlic Skewers 44
  Garlic Lamb Chops 45
  Pork Sausage with Yogurt Dip 45
  Aleppo Pork Kebabs 46
  Easy Pork Tenderloin 47
  Garlic Pork Sirloin Roast 48
  Paprika Pork Tenderloin 49
  Pork Stew 49
  Tender Steak 50
  Meatballs 51
Vegetarian Recipes 52
  Chicken Sandwich 52
  Potato Balls Stuffed with Ham and Cheese 53
  Spring Rolls 54
  Mini Burgers 55
  Sausages And Chorizos 56
  Sausage Puff Pastry 56
  Flank Steak with Balsamic Mustard 57
  Pine Skewers Aceto Reduction 58
  Jacket Potatoes 58
  Stuffed Tomatoes 59
  Parmesan Broccoli 60
  Glazed Carrots 60
  Buttered Zucchini 61
  Sweet & Spicy Parsnips 62
  Tofu in Orange Sauce 63
Seafood Recipes 64
  Salmon Croquettes 64
  Fried Calamari 65
  Soy and Ginger Shrimp 66
  Panko-crusted Tilapia 67

- Potato Crusted Salmon...68
- Snapper Scampi...69
- Thai Fish Cakes with Mango Relish...70
- Tuna Stuffed Potatoes...71
- Baked Tilapia...72
- Lemon Pepper Basa...73
- Ginger Garlic Fish Fillets...74
- Cajun Fish Fillets...75
- Tasty Cajun Salmon...76
- Easy Baked Halibut...77
- Honey Orange Salmon...78
- Blackened Fish Fillets...79

Snacks & Appetizers Recipes...80
- Chicken Sandwich...80
- Potato Balls Stuffed with Ham and Cheese...81
- Spring Rolls...82
- Mini Burgers...83
- Sausages And Chorizos...84
- Sausage Puff Pastry...85
- Flank Steak with Balsamic Mustard...86
- Pine Skewers Aceto Reduction...87
- Spinach Chips...88
- Mozzarella Sticks...89
- Avocado Fries...90
- Pancetta Wrapped Shrimp...91
- Spicy Chicken Wings...92
- Haddock Nuggets...93
- Perfect Crab Dip...94
- Spicy Almonds...95

Desserts Recipes...96
- Apple Rotation...96
- Stuffed brioche crown...97
- Nut cake...98
- Genoise Cake...99
- Frozen Sorrentino gnocchi...100
- Khachapuri (Georgian bread)...100
- Marble cake...101

Apple, cream, and hazelnut crumble 102
Banana Muffins 103
Chocolate Muffins 104
White Chocolate Cheesecake 105

INSTANT OMNI AIR FRYER TOASTER OVEN OVERVIEW

COOKING TIMETABLE

Food	Setting	Cooking Time*	Cooking Temperature*	Accessory & Placement
Thin-cut fries (Frozen)	Air Fry / Roast	14–18 minutes	400°F / 205°C	Air Fryer Basket
Thin-cut fries (Fresh)	Air Fry / Roast	18–20 minutes	400°F / 205°C	Air Fryer Basket
Thick-cut fries (Frozen)	Air Fry / Roast	16–20 minutes	400°F / 205°C	Air Fryer Basket
Thick-cut fries (Fresh)	Air Fry / Roast	20–25 minutes	400°F / 205°C	Air Fryer Basket
Chicken wings (Fresh)	Air Fry / Roast	20–30 minutes	360°F / 182°C	Cooking Tray, Bottom / Air Fryer Basket
Whole chicken (up to 4 lbs)	Roast	50–70 minutes	380°F / 193°C	Rotisserie Spit
Chicken nuggets (Frozen)	Broil	10–15 minutes	400°F / 205°C	Cooking Tray, Middle / Air Fry Basket
Shrimp (Frozen)	Air Fry	8 minutes	400°F / 205°C	Cooking Tray, Middle / Air Fryer Basket
Shrimp (Fresh)	Air Fry	8–10 minutes	350°F / 177°C	Cooking Tray, Middle / Air Fryer Basket
Fish sticks (Frozen)	Broil	8–12 minutes	400°F / 205°C	Cooking Tray, Middle
Asparagus	Broil / Bake	7–9 minutes	370°F / 188°C	Cooking Tray, Middle / Air Fryer Basket
Cauliflower	Broil / Bake	6–10 minutes	370°F / 188°C	Cooking Tray, Middle / Air Fryer Basket

Cake	Bake	25-35 minutes	360°F / 182°C	Cooking Pan, Bottom (Springform Pan)

*Note: *Cooking times and temperatures are recommendations only. Always follow a trusted recipe.*

COOKING WITH THE OMNI TOASTER OVEN

Convection cooking uses rapid air circulation to heat the oven up fast, so food cooks quickly and evenly.

Initial Test Run

Follow these steps to familiarize yourself with the Instant Omni toaster oven and ensure it is operating properly. Once the Initial Test Run has completed, you may use these same steps to start cooking..

1. Open the oven door.

Place the cooking pan on the bottom of the cooking chamber. Close the door.

2. Plug the power cord into a 120V power source.

Display indicates OFF signifying that the oven is in Standby mode.

3. Touch the Air Fry Smart Program key on the display.

Note: *The default Air Fry Smart Program cooking temperature is 400ºF/205ºC.*

4. Turn the Time dial to adjust the cooking time to 20 minutes.

Note: *The cooking temperature and time are preset by the Air Fry Smart Program, however, you can adjust the cooking temperature or time with the Temp and Time dials.*

5. Touch the green Start key to begin. The oven begins Preheat mode and the display indicates On.

6. When the oven reaches the cooking temperature, the cooking time will start to count down on the display.

Note: *For the test run, do not add food to the cooking chamber.*

7. Partway through the Air Fry Smart Program, the oven beeps and indicates turn Food to remind you to turn, flip or rotate your food items.

Open the door to automatically pause the Smart Program, then close the door to resume cooking.

Note: The Smart Program will resume after 10 seconds whether food has been turned or not.

8. The display counts down the last minute of cooking time in seconds.

When the Smart Program is complete, the display indicates End and the fan turns on automatically to cool the oven.

Note: The Omni toaster oven emits a Smart Reminder at 5, 20, and 60 minutes after the Smart Program ends to remind you about your dish.

COOKING TIPS

The Omni toaster oven cooks all your favorite fresh and frozen oven-baked and air-fried snacks—fast!

Use the Smart Programs as a starting point and experiment with cooking times and temperatures to get the results you prefer.

- With the exception of rotisserie-cooked foods, most foods will benefit greatly from a preheated oven.

- When cooking coated food items, choose breadcrumb batters over liquid-based batters to ensure that the batter sticks to the food.

- For crispy, golden fries, soak fresh potato sticks in ice water for 15 minutes, then pat and spray lightly with cooking oil before inserting them into the oven.

- When baking a cake, pie, quiche or any food with filling or batter, use an oven-safe baking dish and cover the food to prevent the top from overcooking.

- Air frying can cause oil and fat to drip from foods. If excessive smoking occurs, carefully remove and empty the cooking pan.

- To ensure seasoning adheres to food items, spray them with cooking oil before adding seasoning.

- Use any oven-safe cookware in your Omni toaster oven.

SMART PROGRAMS

Smart Program	Default Time	Time Range	Default Temperature	Temperature Range	Convection Fan Speed
Air Fry	18 minutes	5 to 45 minutes	400°F/204°C	180-450°F 82-232°C	High
	Ensures the right golden crispiness without the oil.				
Toast	Level 3	Adjusts by quantity	Auto	Darkness Level 1-5	NA
	Select the number of bread or bagel slices to be toasted with the Temp dial, up to a maximum of 6 slices. Adjust your preferred toasting level with the Time dial, from levels 1 to 5. You may adjust the toasting time after the Smart Program has begun.				
Bake	40 minutes	1 minute to 4 hours	350°F/177°C	180-450°F 82-232°C	Low / High
	Perfect for desserts like brownies, cakes and cookies cook quickly and evenly.				
Roast	40 minutes	20 minutes to 4 hours	365°F/185°C	180-450°F 82-232°C	Low / High
	For beautifully roasted meats and vegetables				
Broil	10 minutes	2 to 20 minutes	450°F/232°C	350-450°F 176-232°C	NA
	The direct top-down heat is designed to melt cheese, crisp meat, and caramelize fruits and vegetables.				
Reheat	10 minutes	5 to 60 minutes	300°F/149°C	120-360°F 49-182°C	Low
	Warm up leftovers without overcooking or drying out the food.				

	8 hours	30 minutes to 72 hours	135°F/57°C	85-175°F 29-79°C	Low / High
Dehydrate	Low temperature heat is circulated to effectively draw moisture from foods. Make veggie chips, dehydrated fruit leather and all kinds of delicious jerkies.				

CARE AND CLEANING

Clean the Instant Omni toaster oven after each use. Always unplug the toaster oven and let it cool to room temperature before cleaning. Let all surfaces dry thoroughly before use and before storage.

Part / Accessory	Instructions	Cleaning Method
Cooking Pan	Optionally, prior to use, spray with non-stick cooking spray for easier cleaning.	Dishwasher Safe / Hand Washable
Rotisserie Spit and Forks	Disassemble and clean after each use.	
Rotisserie Lift	Clean as needed.	
Oven Rack	Do not cover the oven rack when cooking.	
Air Fryer Basket	Optionally, spray with non-stick cooking spray before adding food.	
Crumb Tray	Remove and clean after each use and ensure all grease and food debris is fully removed.	
Cooking Chamber	Clean after each use once the cooking chamber is cool. Use a damp cloth or sponge to ensure the heating element, surrounding area and chamber walls are free of grease and food debris. You may use any commercial oven cleaner to remove stubborn grease residue. Use care when cleaning around the bottom heating element	Damp Cloth or Sponge Only
Toaster Oven Exterior	Clean with a soft, damp cloth or sponge, and wipe dry to avoid streaking.	

Note: Never use harsh chemical detergents, scouring pads, or powders on any of the parts or components as this may lead to damage.

To remove baked-on grease residue from accessories and the cooking chamber, unplug the appliance and wait for it to cool. Then spray the affected area with a mixture of baking soda and vinegar, and wipe clean. For stubborn stains, allow the mixture to sit on the affected area for several minutes before removing residue.

BREAKFAST RECIPES

CRISPY POTATO ROSTI

Cooking time: 15 minutes
Serves: 2

Ingredients
- ½ pound russet potatoes, peeled and grated roughly
- 1 tablespoon chives, chopped finely
- 2 tablespoons shallots, minced
- 1/8 cup cheddar cheese
- 3.5 ounces smoked salmon, cut into slices
- 2 tablespoons sour cream
- 1 tablespoon olive oil
- Salt and black pepper, to taste

Directions
1. Preheat the Air fryer to 365 o F and grease a pizza pan with the olive oil.
2. Mix together potatoes, shallots, chives, cheese, salt and black pepper in a large bowl until well combined.
3. Transfer the potato mixture into the prepared pizza pan and place in the Air fryer basket.
4. Cook for about 15 minutes and dish out in a platter.
5. Cut the potato rosti into wedges and top with smoked salmon slices and sour cream to Serves.

TOASTIES AND SAUSAGE IN EGG POND

Cooking time: 22 minutes
Serves: 2

Ingredients

- 3 eggs
- 2 cooked sausages, sliced
- 1 bread slice, cut into sticks
- 1/8 cup mozzarella cheese, grated
- 1/8 cup Parmesan cheese, grated
- ¼ cup cream

Directions

1. Preheat the Air fryer to 365 o F and grease 2 ramekins lightly.
2. Whisk together eggs with cream in a bowl and place in the ramekins.
3. Stir in the bread and sausage slices in the egg mixture and top with cheese.
4. Transfer the ramekins in the Air fryer basket and cook for about 22 minutes.
5. Dish out and Serves warm.

BANANA BREAD

Cooking time: 20 minutes
Serves: 8

Ingredients

- 1 1/3 cups flour
- 1 teaspoon baking soda
- 1 teaspoon baking powder
- ½ cup milk
- 3 bananas, peeled and sliced
- 2/3 cup sugar
- 1 teaspoon ground cinnamon
- 1 teaspoon salt
- ½ cup olive oil

Directions

1. Preheat the Air fryer to 330 o F and grease a loaf pan.

2. Mix together all the dry ingredients with the wet ingredients to form a dough.
3. Place the dough into the prepared loaf pan and transfer into an air fryer basket.
4. Cook for about 20 minutes and remove from air fryer.
5. Cut the bread into desired size slices and Serves warm.

PEANUT BUTTER BANANA BREAD

Cooking time: 40 minutes
Serves: 6

Ingredients
- 1 cup plus 1 tablespoon all-purpose flour
- 1¼ teaspoons baking powder
- 1 large egg
- 2 medium ripe bananas, peeled and mashed
- ¾ cup walnuts, roughly chopped
- ¼ teaspoon salt
- 1/3 cup granulated sugar
- ¼ cup canola oil
- 2 tablespoons creamy peanut butter
- 2 tablespoons sour cream
- 1 teaspoon vanilla extract

Directions
1. Preheat the Air fryer to 330 o F and grease a non-stick baking dish.
2. Mix together the flour, baking powder and salt in a bowl.
3. Whisk together egg with sugar, canola oil, sour cream, peanut butter and vanilla extract in a bowl.
4. Stir in the bananas and beat until well combined.
5. Now, add the flour mixture and fold in the walnuts gently.
6. Mix until combined and transfer the mixture evenly into the prepared baking dish.
7. Arrange the baking dish in an Air fryer basket and cook for about 40 minutes.
8. Remove from the Air fryer and place onto a wire rack to cool.
9. Cut the bread into desired size slices and Serves.

FLAVORFUL BACON CUPS

Cooking time: 15 minutes
Serves: 6
Ingredients
- 6 bacon slices
- 6 bread slices
- 1 scallion, chopped
- 3 tablespoons green bell pepper, seeded and chopped
- 6 eggs
- 2 tablespoons low-fat mayonnaise

Directi o ns
1. Preheat the Air fryer to 375 o F and grease 6 cups muffin tin with cooking spray.
2. Place each bacon slice in a prepared muffin cup.
3. Cut the bread slices with round cookie cutter and place over the bacon slices.
4. Top with bell pepper, scallion and mayonnaise evenly and crack 1 egg in each muffin cup.
5. Place in the Air fryer and cook for about 15 minutes.
6. Dish out and Serves warm.

STYLISH HAM OMELET

Cooking time: 30 minutes
Serves: 2

Ingredients
- 4 small tomatoes, chopped
- 4 eggs
- 2 ham slices
- 1 onion, chopped
- 2 tablespoons cheddar cheese
- Salt and black pepper, to taste

Directions
1. Preheat the Air fryer to 390 o F and grease an Air fryer pan.
2. Place the tomatoes in the Air fryer pan and cook for about 10 minutes.
3. Heat a nonstick skillet on medium heat and add onion and ham.
4. Stir fry for about 5 minutes and transfer into the Air fryer pan.
5. Whisk together eggs, salt and black pepper in a bowl and pour in the Air fryer pan.
6. Set the Air fryer to 335 o F and cook for about 15 minutes.
7. Dish out and Serves warm.

AROMATIC POTATO HASH

Cooking time: 42 minutes
Serves: 4

Ingredients
- 2 teaspoons butter, melted
- 1 medium onion, chopped
- ½ of green bell pepper, seeded and chopped
- 1½ pound russet potatoes, peeled and cubed
- 5 eggs, beaten
- ½ teaspoon dried thyme, crushed
- ½ teaspoon dried savory, crushed
- Salt and black pepper, to taste

Directions
1. Preheat the Air fryer to 390 °F and grease an Air fryer pan with melted butter.
2. Put onion and bell pepper in the Air fryer pan and cook for about 5 minutes.
3. Add the potatoes, thyme, savory, salt and black pepper and cook for about 30 minutes.
4. Meanwhile, heat a greased skillet on medium heat and stir in the beaten eggs.
5. Cook for about 1 minute on each side and remove from the skillet.
6. Cut it into small pieces and transfer the egg pieces into the Air fryer pan.
7. Cook for about 5 more minutes and Serves warm.

HEALTHY TOFU OMELET

Cooking time: 29 minutes
Serves: 2

Ingredients
- ¼ of onion, chopped
- 12-ounce silken tofu, pressed and sliced
- 3 eggs, beaten
- 1 tablespoon chives, chopped
- 1 garlic clove, minced
- 2 teaspoons olive oil
- Salt and black pepper, to taste

Directions
1. Preheat the Air fryer to 355 °F and grease an Air fryer pan with olive oil.
2. Add onion and garlic to the greased pan and cook for about 4 minutes.
3. Add tofu, mushrooms and chives and season with salt and black pepper.
4. Beat the eggs and pour over the tofu mixture.
5. Cook for about 25 minutes, poking the eggs twice in between.
6. Dish out and Serves warm.

SPINACH MUFFINS

Cooking Time: 10 minutes
Serves: 2

Ingredients
- 2 large eggs
- 2 tablespoons heavy cream
- 2 tablespoons frozen spinach, thawed
- 4 teaspoons ricotta cheese, crumbled
- Salt and ground black pepper, as required

Directi o ns
1. Grease 2 ramekins.
2. In each prepared ramekin, crack 1 egg.
3. Divide the cream spinach, cheese, salt and black pepper in each ramekin and gently stir to combine, without breaking the yolks.
4. Arrange a sheet pan in the center of Instant Omni Plus Toaster Oven.
5. Place the muffin molds over the sheet pan.
6. Select "Air Fry" and then adjust the temperature to 330 degrees F.
7. Set the timer for 10 minutes and press "Start".
8. When the display shows "Turn Food" do nothing.
9. When cooking time is complete, remove the muffin molds from Toaster Oven and place the pan onto a wire rack for about 10 minutes.
10. Carefully, invert the muffins onto the platter and Serves warm.

CHICKEN OMELET

Cooking Time: 10 minutes
Serves: 2

Ingredients
- 1 teaspoon olive oil
- 2 scallions, chopped
- ½ jalapeño pepper, seeded and chopped
- 3 eggs
- Salt and ground black pepper, as required
- ¼ cup cooked bacon, chopped

Directi o ns
1. In a frying pan, heat the oil over medium heat and cook the scallion for about 2-3 minutes.
2. Add the jalapeño pepper and cook for about 1 minute.
3. Remove from the heat and set aside to cool slightly.
4. Meanwhile, in a bowl, add the eggs, salt, and black pepper and beat well.
5. Add the scallion mixture and chicken and stir to combine.
6. Place the chicken mixture into a small baking dish.
7. Arrange the baking dish in the center of Instant Omni Plus Toaster Oven.
8. Select "Air Fry" and then adjust the temperature to 355 degrees F.
9. Set the timer for 6 minutes and press "Start".
10. When the display shows "Turn Food" do nothing.
11. When cooking time is complete, remove the baking dish from Toaster Oven.
12. Cut the omelet into 2 portions and Serves hot.

TOFU & MUSHROOM OMELET

Cooking Time: 33 minutes
Serves: 2

Ingredients
- 2 teaspoons canola oil
- ¼ of onion, chopped
- 1 garlic clove, minced
- 8 ounces silken tofu, drained, pressed and sliced
- 3½ ounces fresh mushrooms, sliced
- Salt and freshly ground black pepper, as needed
- 3 eggs, beaten

Directi o ns
1. In a frying pan, heat the oil over medium heat and sauté the onion and garlic for about 3-4 minutes.
2. Add the mushrooms and cook for about 3-4 minutes.
3. Stir in the mushrooms, salt and black pepper and remove from the heat.
4. Transfer the mixture into a baking dish.
5. Arrange the baking dish in the center of Instant Omni Plus Toaster Oven.
6. Select "Air Fry" and then adjust the temperature to 355 degrees F.
7. Set the timer for 25 minutes and press "Start".
8. When the display shows "Turn Food" stir the mixture.
9. When cooking time is complete, remove the baking dish from Toaster Oven.
10. Cut the omelet into 2 portions and Serves hot

BACON, KALE & TOMATO FRITTATA

Cooking Time: 16 minutes
Serves: 2

Ingredients
- ¼ cup bacon, chopped
- ¼ cup fresh kale, tough ribs removed and chopped
- ½ of tomato, cubed
- 3 eggs
- Salt and ground black pepper, as required
- ¼ cup Parmesan cheese, grated

Directions
1. Heat a nonstick skillet over medium heat and cook the bacon for about 5 minutes.
2. Add the kale and cook for about 1-2 minutes.
3. Add the tomato and cook for about 2-3 minutes.
4. Remove from the heat and drain the grease from skillet.
5. Set aside to cool slightly.
6. Meanwhile, in a small bowl, add the eggs, salt and black pepper and beat well.
7. In a greased baking dish, place the bacon mixture and top with the eggs, followed by the cheese.
8. Arrange the baking dish in the center of Instant Omni Plus Toaster Oven.
9. Select "Air Fry" and then adjust the temperature to 355 degrees F.
10. Set the timer for 8 minutes and press "Start".
11. When the display shows "Turn Food" do nothing.
12. When cooking time is complete, remove the baking dish from Toaster Oven.
13. Cut into equal-sized wedges and Serves.

TOMATO QUICHE

Cooking Time: 30 minutes
Serves: 2

Ingredients

- 4 eggs
- ¼ cup scallion, chopped
- ½ cup fresh plum tomatoes, chopped
- ½ cup unsweetened almond milk
- 1 cup Cheddar cheese, shredded
- Salt and freshly ground black pepper, as required

Directions

1. In a small baking dish, add all the ingredients and mix well.
2. Arrange the baking dish in the center of Instant Omni Plus Toaster Oven.
3. Select "Air Fry" and then adjust the temperature to 340 degrees F.
4. Set the timer for 30 minutes and press "Start".
5. When the display shows "Turn Food" do nothing.
6. When cooking time is complete, remove the baking dish from Toaster Oven.
7. Cut into equal-sized wedges and Serves.

POULTRY RECIPES

SIMPLE ROASTED CHICKEN

Cooking Time: 40 minutes
Serves: 3
Ingredients
- 1 (1½-pounds) whole chicken
- Salt and ground black pepper, as required

Directions
1. Season the chicken with salt and black pepper.
2. Arrange the chicken into the greased air fryer basket, breast-side down.
3. Arrange the fryer basket in the center of Instant Omni Plus Toaster Oven.
4. Select "Air Fry" and then adjust the temperature to 390 degrees F.
5. Set the timer for 40 minutes and press "Start".
6. When the display shows "Turn Food" do nothing.
7. When cooking time is complete, remove the air fryer basket from Toaster Oven.
8. Place the chicken onto a platter for about 5-10 minutes before carving.
9. With a sharp knife, cut the chicken into desired sized pieces and Serves.

MARINATED CHICKEN LEGS

Cooking Time: 20 minutes
Serves: 4

Ingredients
- 4 (8-ounce) chicken legs
- 2 tablespoons balsamic vinegar
- 2 teaspoons garlic, minced
- Salt, as required
- 4 tablespoons plain Greek yogurt
- 1 teaspoon red chili powder
- 1 teaspoon ground cumin
- 1 teaspoon ground coriander
- Ground black pepper, as required

Directions
1. In a bowl, add the chicken legs, vinegar, garlic and salt and mix well.
2. Set aside for about 15 minutes.
3. Meanwhile, in another bowl, mix together the yogurt, spices, salt and black pepper.
4. Add the chicken legs into bowl and coat with the spice mixture generously.
5. Cover the bowl of chicken and refrigerate for at least 10-12 hours.
6. Arrange the chicken legs into the greased air fryer basket.
7. Arrange the fryer basket in the center of Instant Omni Plus Toaster Oven.
8. Select "Air Fry" and then adjust the temperature to 445 degrees F.
9. Set the timer for 20 minutes and press "Start".
10. When the display shows "Turn Food" do nothing.
11. When cooking time is complete, remove the air fryer basket from Toaster Oven.
12. Serves hot.

SPICY CHICKEN THIGHS

Cooking Time: 20 minutes
Serves: 4

Ingredients
- 4 (4-ounces) skinless, boneless chicken thighs
- ½ teaspoon cayenne pepper
- ½ teaspoon paprika
- ½ teaspoon ground cumin
- Salt and ground black pepper, as required
- 2 tablespoons olive oil

Directions
1. In a bowl, mix together the spices, salt and black pepper.
2. Rub the chicken thighs with spice mixture evenly and then, brush with melted butter.
3. Place the chicken thighs into a greased baking pan.
4. Arrange the drip pan in the bottom of Instant Omni Plus Toaster Oven.
5. Place the baking pan over the drip pan.
6. Select "Bake" and then adjust the temperature to 450 degrees F.
7. Set the timer for 20 minutes and press "Start".
8. When the display shows "Add Food" place the baking pan over the drip pan.
9. When the display shows "Turn Food" do nothing.
10. When cooking time is complete, remove the pan from Toaster Oven.
11. Serves hot.

CRISPY CHICKEN DRUMSTICKS

Cooking Time: 25 minutes   Serves: 4

Ingredients
- 4 chicken drumsticks
- 1 tablespoon adobo seasoning
- Salt, as required
- 1 tablespoon onion powder
- 1 tablespoon garlic powder
- ½ tablespoon paprika
- Ground black pepper, as required
- 2 eggs
- 2 tablespoons milk
- 1 cup all-purpose flour
- ¼ cup cornstarch

Directions
1. Season chicken drumsticks with adobo seasoning and a pinch of salt.
2. Set aside for about 5minutes.
3. In a small bowl, add the spices, salt and black pepper and mix well.
4. In a shallow bowl, add the eggs, milk and 1 teaspoon of spice mixture and beat until well combined.
5. In another shallow bowl, add the flour, cornstarch and remaining spice mixture.
6. Coat the chicken drumsticks with flour mixture and tap off the excess.
7. Now, dip the chicken drumsticks in egg mixture
8. Again, coat the chicken drumsticks with flour mixture.
9. Arrange the chicken drumsticks onto a wire rack lined baking sheet and set aside for about 15 minutes.
10. Now, arrange the chicken drumsticks onto a sheet pan and spray the chicken with cooking spray lightly.
11. Arrange the sheet pan in the center of Instant Omni Plus Toaster Oven.
12. Select "Air Fry" and then adjust the temperature to 350 degrees F.
13. Set the timer for 25 minutes and press "Start".
14. When the display shows "Turn Food" do nothing.
15. When cooking time is complete, remove the air fryer basket from Toaster Oven.
16. Serves hot.

SWEET & SPICY CHICKEN DRUMSTICKS

Cooking Time: 20 minutes
Serves: 4

Ingredients
- 1 garlic clove, crushed
- 1 teaspoon cayenne pepper
- 2 teaspoons brown sugar
- 1 tablespoon Dijon mustard
- Salt and ground black pepper, as required
- 1 tablespoon olive oil
- 4 (6-ounce) chicken drumsticks

Directions
1. In a bowl, mix together all ingredients except chicken drumsticks.
2. Rub the chicken with the oil mix and refrigerate to marinate for about 20-30 minutes.
3. Place the chicken drumsticks onto a greased sheet pan.
4. Arrange the sheet pan in the center of Instant Omni Plus Toaster Oven.
5. Select "Air Fry" and then adjust the temperature to 390 degrees F.
6. Set the timer for 10 minutes and press "Start".
7. When the display shows "Turn Food" arrange the chicken, breast-side up.
8. Now, adjust the temperature to 300 degrees F.
9. Set the timer for 10 minutes and press "Start".
10. When the display shows "Turn Food" do nothing.
11. When cooking time is complete, remove the sheet pan from Toaster Oven.
12. Serves hot.

CRISPY CHICKEN BREAST

Cooking Time: 40 minutes
Serves: 3

Ingredients
- ¼ cup all-purpose flour
- 1 large egg, beaten
- ¼ cup fresh parsley, chopped
- 1 cup seasoned breadcrumbs
- 3 (5-ounce) boneless, skinless chicken breasts

Directions
1. In a shallow, dish place the flour.
2. In a second shallows dish, mix together the egg and parsley.
3. In a third shallow dish, place breadcrumbs.
4. Coat the chicken breasts with flour, then dip into eggs and finally coat with breadcrumbs.
5. Place the chicken breasts onto a greased sheet pan.
6. Arrange the drip pan in the bottom of Instant Omni Plus Toaster Oven.
7. Place the sheet pan over the drip pan.
8. Select "Roast" and then adjust the temperature to 375 degrees F.
9. Set the timer for 40 minutes and press "Start".
10. When the display shows "Turn Food" do nothing.
11. When cooking time is complete, remove the sheet pan from Toaster Oven.
12. Serves hot.

BUTTERED TURKEY WINGS

Cooking Time: 26 minutes
Serves: 4

Ingredients
- 2 pounds turkey wings
- Salt and ground black pepper, as required
- 3 tablespoons butter, melted

Directions
1. In a large bowl, add the turkey wings, butter, salt and black pepper and mix well.
2. Arrange the turkey wings into the greased air fryer basket in a single layer.
3. Arrange the fryer basket in the center of Instant Omni Plus Toaster Oven.
4. Select "Air Fry" and then adjust the temperature to 380 degrees F.
5. Set the timer for 26 minutes and press "Start".
6. Meanwhile, in another large bowl, mix together the remaining ingredients.
7. When the display shows "Turn Food" flip the turkey wings.
8. When cooking time is complete, remove the air fryer basket from Toaster Oven.
9. Serves hot.

ROSEMARY TURKEY BREAST

Cooking Time: 1 hour 20 minutes

Serves: 6

Ingredients
- 1 (2¾-pound) bone-in, skin-on turkey breast half
- 2 tablespoons fresh rosemary, minced
- Salt and ground black pepper, as required

Directi o ns
1. Rub the turkey breast with the rosemary, salt and black pepper evenly.
2. Arrange the turkey breast onto a greased baking pan.
3. Arrange the drip pan in the bottom of Instant Omni Plus Toaster Oven.
4. Place the baking pan over the drip pan.
5. Select "Bake" and then adjust the temperature to 450 degrees F.
6. Set the timer for 1 hour 20 minutes and press "Start".
7. When the display shows "Turn Food" flip the turkey wings.
8. When cooking time is complete, remove the air baking pan from Toaster Oven.
9. Place the turkey breast onto a cutting board.
10. With a piece of foil, cover the turkey breast for about 20 minutes before slicing.
11. With a sharp knife, cut the turkey breast into desired size slices and Serves.

GREEK CHICKEN THIGHS

Cooking Time: 55 minutes
Serves: 4

Ingredients
- 8 chicken thighs
- 3 tbsp fresh parsley, chopped
- 2 cups grape tomatoes
- 1 1/2 lbs potatoes, cut into small chunks
- 4 tbsp olive oil
- 1 tsp dried oregano
- 6 garlic cloves, crushed
- 1/4 cup capers, drained
- 10 oz jar roasted red peppers, drained and sliced
- Pepper
- Salt

Directi o ns
1. Season chicken with pepper and salt.
2. Heat 2 tablespoons of olive oil in a pan over medium heat.
3. Add chicken to the pan and sear until lightly golden brown from all the sides.
4. Transfer chicken onto a cooking pan.
5. Add tomato, potatoes, capers, oregano, garlic, and red peppers around the chicken.
6. Season with pepper and salt and drizzle with remaining olive oil.
7. Select bake mode and set the omni to 400 F for 55 minutes once the oven beeps, place the cooking pan into the oven.
8. Garnish with parsley and Serves.

BAKED DILL FETA CHICKEN

Cooking Time: 35 minutes
Serves: 4

Ingredients
- 2 lbs chicken tenders
- 2 tbsp olive oil
- 3 dill sprigs
- 1 large zucchini
- 1 cup grape tomatoes

For topping:
- 2 tbsp feta cheese, crumbled
- 1 tbsp olive oil
- 1 tbsp fresh lemon juice
- 1 tbsp fresh dill, chopped

Directions
1. Drizzle oil on a cooking pan then place chicken, zucchini, dill, and tomatoes on the tray. Season with salt.
2. Select bake mode and set the omni to 400 F for 30 minutes once the oven beeps, place the cooking pan into the oven.
3. Meanwhile, in a small bowl, stir together all topping ingredients.
4. Place chicken on the serving tray then top with vegetables and discard dill sprigs.
5. Sprinkle topping mixture on top of chicken and vegetables.
6. Serves and enjoy.

LEMON GARLIC CHICKEN

Cooking Time: 40 minutes
Serves: 4

Ingredients
- 2 lbs chicken drumsticks
- 2 tbsp parsley, chopped
- 1 fresh lemon juice
- 8 garlic cloves, sliced
- 2 tbsp olive oil
- Pepper
- Salt

Directions
1. Spray a cooking pan with cooking spray.
2. Place chicken on the cooking pan. Season chicken with pepper and salt.
3. Sprinkle the parsley and garlic over the chicken. Drizzle with lemon juice and olive oil.
4. Select bake mode and set the omni to 450 F for 40 minutes once the oven beeps, place the cooking pan into the oven.
5. Serves and enjoy.

DELICIOUS CHICKEN TENDERS

Cooking Time: 20 minutes
Serves: 4

Ingredients
- 1 lbs chicken tenders
- 1 garlic clove, minced
- 1/2 oz fresh lemon juice
- 2 tbsp fresh tarragon, chopped
- 1/2 cup whole grain mustard
- 1/2 tsp paprika
- 1/2 tsp pepper
- 1/4 tsp kosher salt

Directions
1. Add all ingredients except chicken to the large bowl and mix well.
2. Add chicken to the bowl and stir until well coated.
3. Place chicken on a baking dish and cover dish with foil.
4. Select bake mode and set the omni to 425 F for 20 minutes once the oven beeps, place the baking dish into the oven.
5. Serves and enjoy.

HERB CHICKEN THIGHS

Cooking Time: 25 minutes
Serves: 2

Ingredients
- 1 lb chicken thighs
- 2 tbsp lemon juice
- 1/8 tsp thyme, dried
- 1/2 tsp fresh rosemary, chopped
- 1 tsp garlic, minced
- 2 tbsp white wine
- 1/2 cup tangerine juice
- Black pepper
- Salt

Directions
1. Place chicken thighs into the bowl.
2. In another bowl, mix together tangerine juice, garlic, white wine, lemon juice, thyme, rosemary, pepper, and salt.
3. Pour over chicken thighs and place them in the refrigerator for 20 minutes.
4. Spray cooking pan with cooking spray.
5. Arrange marinated chicken on cooking pan.
6. Select bake mode and set the omni to 450 F for 25 minutes once the oven beeps, place the cooking pan into the oven.
7. Serves and enjoy.

EASY CHILI GARLIC CHICKEN WINGS

Cooking Time: 60 minutes
Serves: 4

Ingredients
- 2 lbs chicken wings
- 1/8 tsp paprika
- 2 tsp seasoned salt
- 1/2 cup coconut flour
- 1/4 tsp garlic powder
- 1/4 tsp chili powder

Directions
1. In a mixing bowl, add all ingredients except chicken wings and mix well.
2. Add chicken wings to the bowl and coat well and place it on a cooking pan.
3. Select bake mode and set the omni to 400 F for 60 minutes once the oven beeps, place the cooking pan into the oven.
4. Serves and enjoy.

CHICKEN CASSEROLE

Cooking Time: 35 minutes
Serves: 8

Ingredients
- 2 1/2 lbs chicken breasts, boneless and cubed
- 12 oz roasted red peppers, drained and chopped
- 1 tsp xanthan gum
- 1 tbsp tomato paste
- 5.4 oz coconut cream
- 10 garlic cloves
- 2/3 cup mayonnaise
- 5 zucchini, cut into cubes
- 1 tsp salt

Directions
1. Add zucchini and chicken to a casserole dish. Cover dish with foil.
2. Select bake mode and set the omni to 400 F for 25 minutes once the oven beeps, place casserole dish into the oven.
3. Stir well and cook for 10 minutes more.
4. Meanwhile, in a bowl, stir together the remaining ingredients.
5. Pour bowl mixture over chicken and zucchini.
6. Serves and enjoy.

MEAT RECIPES

PROVENCAL PORK

Cooking Time: 15 minutes
Serves: 2

Ingredients
- 1 red onion, sliced
- 1 yellow bell pepper, cut into strips
- 1 green bell pepper, cut into strips
- Salt and black pepper, to taste
- 2 teaspoons Provencal herbs
- ½ teaspoon mustard
- 1 tablespoon olive oil
- 7 ounces pork tenderloin

Directions
1. In a dish, mix salt, pepper, onion, green bell pepper, yellow bell pepper, half the oil, and herbs and toss well.
2. Season pork with mustard, salt, pepper, and rest of the oil. Toss well and add to vegetables.
3. Cook in the air fryer at 370F for 15 minutes.
4. Serves.

LAMB WITH BRUSSELS SPROUTS

Cooking Time: 1 hour and 10 minutes
Serves: 2

Ingredients
- 1 pound leg of lamb, scored
- 1 tablespoon olive oil
- ½ tablespoon rosemary, chopped
- ½ tablespoon lemon thyme, chopped
- 1 clove garlic, minced
- ¾ pound brussels sprouts, trimmed
- ½ tablespoon butter, melted
- ¼ cup sour cream
- Salt and black pepper, to taste

Directions
1. Season the leg of lamb with rosemary, thyme, salt, and pepper. Brush with oil, and place in the air fryer basket.
2. Cook at 300F for 1 hour. Transfer to a plate and keep warm.
3. In a pan, mix brussels sprouts with sour cream, butter, garlic, salt, and pepper. Mix well and cook at 400F for 10 minutes.
4. Divide lamb on plates, add Brussels sprouts on the side and Serves.

ZESTY PORK SKEWERS

Cooking time: 20 minutes
Serves: 4

Ingredients

- 2 teaspoons ground cumin
- 2 teaspoons ground coriander
- 1 onion, cut into pieces
- 1/4 teaspoon ground cinnamon
- 1/8 teaspoon ground smoked paprika
- 2 teaspoons orange zest
- 1/2 yellow bell pepper, sliced into squares
- 1/2 teaspoon salt
- 1/2 teaspoon black pepper
- 1 tablespoon lemon juice
- 2 teaspoons olive oil
- 1 1/2 lbs. (680.389g) Pork, cubed

Directions

1. Toss pork with the rest of the skewer's ingredients in a bowl.
2. Thread the pork and veggies on the skewers alternately.
3. Place these pork skewers in the air fry basket.
4. Press "power button" of air fry oven and turn the dial to select the "air fryer" mode.
5. Press the time button and again turn the dial to set the cooking time to 20 minutes.
6. Now push the temp button and rotate the dial to set the temperature at 370 degrees f.
7. Once preheated, place the air fryer basket in the oven and close its lid.
8. Flip the skewers when cooked halfway through then resume cooking.
9. Serves warm.

BEEF STRIPS WITH VEGETABLES

Cooking Time: 22 minutes
Serves: 2

Ingredients
- 2 beef steaks, cut into strips
- Salt and black pepper, to taste
- 7 ounces of snow peas
- 8 ounces white mushrooms, halved
- 1 yellow onion, cut into rings
- 2 tablespoons soy sauce
- 1 teaspoon olive oil

Directions
1. In a bowl, mix soy sauce and olive oil, and whisk. Add beef strips and coat.
2. In another bowl, mix mushrooms, onion, snow peas with salt, pepper, and oil. Toss well.
3. Place in pan and cook in the air fryer at 350F for 16 minutes.
4. Add beef strips to the pan as well and cook at 400F for 6 minutes more.
5. Serves.

PORK GARLIC SKEWERS

Cooking time: 20 minutes
Serves: 4

Ingredients
- 1 lb. (453.592g) Pork, boned and diced
- 1 lemon, juiced and chopped
- 3 tablespoon olive oil
- 20 garlic cloves, chopped
- 1 handful rosemary, chopped
- 3 green peppers, cubed
- 2 red onions, cut into wedges

Directi o ns
1. Toss the pork with the rest of the skewer's ingredients in a bowl.
2. Thread the pork, peppers, garlic, and onion on the skewers, alternately.
3. Place these pork skewers in the air fry basket.
4. Press "power button" of air fry oven and turn the dial to select the "air fryer" mode.
5. Press the time button and again turn the dial to set the cooking time to 20 minutes.
6. Now push the temp button and rotate the dial to set the temperature at 370 degrees f.
7. Once preheated, place the air fryer basket in the oven and close its lid.
8. Flip the skewers when cooked halfway through then resume cooking.
9. Serves warm.

GARLIC LAMB CHOPS

Cooking Time: 10 minutes
Serves: 2

Ingredients
- 1 ½ tablespoon olive oil
- 4 lamb chops
- Salt and black pepper, to taste
- 2 cloves garlic, minced
- ½ tablespoons oregano, chopped
- ½ tablespoon coriander, chopped

Directions
1. In a bowl, mix oregano with garlic, oil, salt, pepper, and lamb chops and coat well.
2. Cook in the air fryer at 400F for 10 minutes.
3. Serves.

PORK SAUSAGE WITH YOGURT DIP

Cooking time: 10 minutes
Serves: 8

Ingredients
- 2 tablespoon cumin seed
- 2 tablespoon coriander seed
- 2 tablespoon fennel seed
- 1 tablespoon paprika
- 4 garlic cloves, minced
- ½ teaspoon ground cinnamon
- 1 ½ lb. (680.389g) Lean minced pork

For the yogurt
- 3 zucchinis, grated
- 2 teaspoon cumin seed, toasted
- 9 oz. Greek yogurt
- Small handful chopped the coriander
- A small handful of chopped mint

Directi o ns
1. Blend all the spices and seeds with garlic and cinnamon in a blender.
2. Add this spice paste to the minced pork then mix well.
3. Make 8 sausages and thread each on the skewers.
4. Place these pork skewers in the air fry basket.
5. Press "power button" of air fry oven and turn the dial to select the "air fryer" mode.
6. Press the time button and again turn the dial to set the cooking time to 10 minutes.
7. Now push the temp button and rotate the dial to set the temperature at 370 degrees f.
8. Once preheated, place the air fryer basket in the oven and close its lid.
9. Flip the skewers when cooked halfway through then resume cooking.
10. Prepare the yogurt ingredients in a bowl.
11. Serves skewers with the yogurt mixture.

ALEPPO PORK KEBABS

Cooking time: 16 minutes
Serves: 6
Ingredients
- Pork kebabs
- 1 lb. (453.592g) Ground pork
- 1/2 an onion, finely diced
- 3 garlic cloves, finely minced
- 2 teaspoons cumin
- 2 teaspoons coriander
- 2 teaspoons sumac
- 1 teaspoon Aleppo chili flakes
- 1 ½ teaspoons salt
- 2 tablespoons chopped mint

Directi o ns
1. Toss pork with the rest of the kebob ingredients in a bowl.
2. Make 6 sausages out of this mince and thread them on the skewers.

3. Place these pork skewers in the air fry basket.
4. Press "power button" of air fry oven and turn the dial to select the "air fryer" mode.
5. Press the time button and again turn the dial to set the cooking time to 16 minutes.
6. Now push the temp button and rotate the dial to set the temperature at 370 degrees f.
7. Once preheated, place the air fryer basket in the oven and close its lid.
8. Flip the skewers when cooked halfway through then resume cooking.
9. Serves the skewers with yogurt sauce.

EASY PORK TENDERLOIN

Cooking Time: 35 minutes
Serves: 6

Ingredients
- 2 lbs pork tenderloin
- 2 garlic cloves, chopped
- Pepper
- Salt

For the spice mix:
- 1/2 tsp allspice
- 1 tsp cinnamon
- 1 tsp cumin
- 1 tsp coriander
- 1/4 tsp cayenne
- 1 tsp oregano
- 1/4 tsp cloves

Directions
1. In a small bowl, mix together all spice ingredients and set aside.
2. Using a sharp knife make slits on pork tenderloin and insert garlic into each slit.
3. Rub spice mixture over pork tenderloin. Sprinkle with pepper and salt.

4. Spray cooking pan with cooking spray.
5. Place pork tenderloin on cooking pan.
6. Select bake mode and set the omni to 375 F for 35 minutes once the oven beeps, place the cooking pan into the oven.
7. Slice and Serves.

GARLIC PORK SIRLOIN ROAST

Cooking Time: 1 hour 15 minutes
Serves: 4

Ingredients
- 2 lbs pork sirloin roast
- 2 tbsp olive oil
- 4 garlic cloves, sliced
- 1/2 tsp pepper
- 1 tsp salt

Directi o ns
1. Using a sharp knife make slits on top of roast and stuff sliced garlic in each slit. Season pork roast with pepper and salt.
2. Heat olive oil in a pan over medium-high heat.
3. Place roast on the hot pan and cook until brown from all the sides.
4. Transfer pork roast on a cooking pan.
5. Select bake mode and set the omni to 350 F for 60-70 minutes once the oven beeps, place cooking pan into the oven. Turn roast halfway through.
6. Slice and Serves.

PAPRIKA PORK TENDERLOIN

Cooking Time: 30 minutes
Serves: 6
Ingredients
- 2 lbs pork tenderloin

For rub:
- 1 tbsp smoked paprika
- 1 tbsp garlic powder
- 1 tbsp onion powder
- 1/2 tsp salt

Directions
1. In a small bowl, combine together all rub ingredients.
2. Coat pork tenderloin with the rub.
3. Heat ovenproof pan over medium-high heat. Spray pan with cooking spray. Sear pork on all sides until lightly golden brown.
4. Select bake mode and set the omni to 425 F for 30 minutes once the oven beeps, place the pan into the oven.
5. Slice and Serves.

PORK STEW

Cooking Time: 8 hours 10 minutes
Serves: 4
Ingredients
- 4 pork chops, boneless
- 1/2 cup olives
- 2 yellow bell pepper, sliced
- 2 red bell peppers, sliced
- 1 onion, sliced

- 2 tsp garlic, minced
- 1 tbsp olive oil
- 2 tsp chili, diced
- 1 bay leaf
- 2 1/4 cups vegetable stock
- 14 oz can tomatoes, chopped

Directions
1. Heat olive oil in a pan over medium heat.
2. Add garlic, chili, and onion to the pan and sauté for 5 minutes.
3. Add pork chops to the pan and cook for 5 minutes.
4. Transfer pan mixture to the Dutch oven along with remaining ingredients and stir well.
5. Cover and place in omni toaster oven.
6. Select slow cook mode and set the omni to low for 8 hours. Press start.
7. Stir and Serves.

TENDER STEAK

Cooking Time: 12 minutes
Serves: 2

Ingredients
- 2 ribeye steak
- 2 tbsp fresh parsley, chopped
- 1 stick butter, softened
- 1 tsp Worcestershire sauce
- 2 tsp garlic, minced
- Pepper
- Salt

Directions
1. In a bowl, mix together butter, Worcestershire sauce, garlic, parsley, and salt and place in the refrigerator.
2. Season steak with pepper and salt.
3. Spray air-fryer basket with cooking spray.

4. Place seasoned steak in the preheated air fryer basket.
5. Place air fryer basket into the oven and select air fry mode set omni to the 400 F for 12 minutes.
6. Remove steak from oven and top with butter mixture.
7. Serves and enjoy.

MEATBALLS

Cooking Time: 20 minutes
Serves: 12

Ingredients
- 1 lb ground beef
- 1/4 cup onion, chopped
- 3 tbsp mushrooms, chopped
- 2 tbsp fresh parsley, chopped
- 1/2 cup almond flour
- 1/2 tsp pepper
- 1 tsp salt

Directions
1. In a bowl, mix together ground beef, parsley, onions, and mushrooms.
2. Add remaining ingredients and mix until well combined.
3. Make small balls from the mixture.
4. Spray air fryer basket with cooking spray. Place prepared meatballs in the air fryer basket.
5. Place air fryer basket into the oven and select air fry mode set omni to the 350 F for 20 minutes.
6. Serves and enjoy.

VEGETARIAN RECIPES

CHICKEN SANDWICH

Cooking time: 15 minutes.
Serves: 2
Ingredients
- 2 cloves garlic
- Fresh parsley leaves
- 500g chopped breast
- 1 tsp Salt
- Pepper
- 1 egg L
- 50g milk
- 50g Cheese spread
- 14-16 slices sliced bread
- 7-8 slices semi-cured cheese

Directi o ns
1. Chop the garlic and parsley.
2. Add the breast in pieces, salt, and pepper
3. Add the rest of the ingredients and spread slices!
4. Spread the paste on all the slices, cover half with a slice of cheese, and cover with another slice, cut into triangles and there are two options, pass them by egg and breadcrumbs
5. Preheat the 2200C air fryer, about 8 or 10 minutes, until the bread becomes colored.

POTATO BALLS STUFFED WITH HAM AND CHEESE

Cooking time: 25 minutes.
Serves: 4

Ingredients
- 4 potatoes
- 100g cooked ham
- 100g of grated or grated cheese
- Salt
- Ground pepper
- Flour
- Oil

Directi o ns
1. Peel the potatoes and cut into quarters.
2. Put in a pot with water and bring to the fire, let cook until tender.
3. Drain and squeeze with a fork until the potatoes are made dough and season.
4. Add the ham and cheese.
5. Let's link everything.
6. Make balls and pass through the flour.
7. Spray with oil and go to the basket of the air fryer.
8. Select 20 minutes, 2000C for each batch of balls you put. Do not pile up because they would break down. From time to time remove from the basket so that they are made on all sides, you have to shake the basket so that the balls roll a little and Serves.

SPRING ROLLS

Cooking time: 30 minutes.
Serves: 6

Ingredients
- 8 sheets of Philo pasta
- 2 onions
- 2 carrots
- 1 piece of Chinese cabbage
- 75g of bean sprouts
- Salt
- Ground pepper
- Extra virgin olive oil
- 1 dash of soy sauce

Directions
1. Grate the carrots, cabbage, and onions.
2. Put in the Wok some extra virgin olive oil.
3. When it's hot, add the vegetables,
4. Season and sauté without losing the crunchy touch.
5. Incorporate the bean sprouts and the soy sauce.
6. Sauté and let temper so that the Philo pasta does not get very wet.
7. Extend the sheets, distribute the filling between the layers and roll up, in the form of a roll, that is, the filling in the center of the sheet. Give the first fold from the bottom up, then the sides mount them on top of each other, and now you end up spinning up its width.
8. Place in the basket of the air fryer, 2 in 2.
9. Paint with oil.
10. Select 20 minutes, 180oC.
11. Make all the rolls.
12. When you have them all done, place all in the basket of the air fryer, one over the other carefully. Select 5 minutes, 180oC, and give a heat stroke so that all are Servesd hot.

MINI BURGERS

Cooking time: 25 minutes.
Serves: 4

Ingredients
- 500g Minced pork
- Salt
- Ground pepper
- Garlic Powder
- Fresh parsley
- Spices
- 1 egg
- 1 tbsp grated bread
- Mini Bread for Burgers

Directi o ns
1. Dress the meat of the hamburgers.
2. Add some salt to the ground beef, some ground pepper, garlic powder, a tablespoon of chopped fresh parsley, a teaspoon of spices.
3. Now, throw an egg and one or two teaspoons of breadcrumbs, so that the meat becomes more consistent. Stir all ingredients well until everything is integrated
4. Then, cover it with transparent and let it rest in the refrigerator for at least half an hour or more. It will be easier after handling the meat and giving it the shape of a hamburger.
5. Once the time has elapsed, take out the meat. Take it out of the paper that surrounds the container and begins to mold and make the mini burger.
6. To prepare them in the fryer:
7. First, heat the fryer. So, adjust the thermostat to 200ºC and the timer for about 5 minutes. When it is hot, the pilot or the green light will go out.
8. When half the time has passed, turn around so that they are done well by both parties.

SAUSAGES AND CHORIZOS

Cooking time: 20 minutes.
Serves: 2-4

Ingredients
- 300g of sausage or frozen sausages
- One tablespoon olive oil

Directions
1. Remove sausages directly from the freezer and place them in the fryer basket.
2. To defrost sausages and remove some of their fat, you must boil them for 5 to 10 minutes, and then prick food to remove all the remaining fat.
3. Then separate the sausages and chorizos on a tray or bowl.
4. Add a tablespoon of your favorite oil (preferably olive oil) in the bowl and mix the sausage well with the oil.
5. Then place the sausages and chorizos in the fryer basket.
6. Program your fryer at a temperature of 190°C and the timer in about 10 minutes.
7. Then turn the sausage as well as chorizos and perform the same process with the fryer.
8. And finally, after 10 minutes, Serves and enjoy them.

SAUSAGE PUFF PASTRY

Cooking time: 20 minutes.
Serves: 1-4

Ingredients
- Amount needed of puff pastry
- Amount needed of sausages

Directions
1. Cut the puff pastry into thin slices about 5 cm wide.

2. Divide the sausages into two pieces.
3. Preheat the air fryer a few minutes at 180oC.
4. Meanwhile, roll each piece of sausage with a strip of puff pastry and paint on top with beaten egg.
5. Place in the basket of the air fryer.
6. Set the timer 10 minutes at 180oC temperature.
7. Take as an appetizer at any time of the year. Kids love it.

FLANK STEAK WITH BALSAMIC MUSTARD

Cooking time: 2h 15 minutes.
Serves: 3

Ingredients
- 60 ml of olive oil
- 60 ml balsamic vinegar
- 36g Dijon mustard
- 16 oz flank steak
- Salt and pepper to taste
- 4 basil leaves, sliced

Directi o ns
1. Mix olive oil, balsamic vinegar, and mustard. Mix them to create a marinade.
2. Put the steak directly in the marinade. Cover with plastic wrap and marinate in the fridge for 2 hours or at night.
3. Remove from the refrigerator and let it reach room temperature.
4. Preheat the air fryer by pressing Start/Pause.
5. Place the fillet in the preheated air fryer, select Fillet, and press Start/Pause.
6. Cut the steak at an angle through the muscle. Season with salt and pepper and decorate with the basil to Serves.

PINE SKEWERS ACETO REDUCTION

Cooking time: 15 minutes.
Serves: 2

Ingredients
- 1 small can of pineapple in its juice
- Necessary quantity Peeled prawns
- Skewers Sticks
- For the sauce:
- 150 ml of Balsamic Aceto
- 120g of sugar

Directions
1. Open a small can of pineapple in its juice and drain well.
2. Cut the pineapple slices into four parts and set aside.
3. Peel the prawns and take out the tail.
4. Preheat the air fryer at 1800C temperature for a few minutes and put the skewers in the basket. Program the timer about 10 minutes at 18000C.
5. To prepare the balsamic Aceto sauce: place the Aceto and sugar in a small pot. Reduce over low heat until it thickens but without letting caramel.
6. Let stand until it cools.

JACKET POTATOES

Cooking Time: 20 minutes
Serves: 2

Ingredients
- 2 potatoes
- 1 tablespoon mozzarella cheese, shredded
- 3 tablespoons sour cream
- 1 tablespoon butter, softened
- 1 teaspoon chives, minced
- Salt and ground black pepper, as required

Directions
1. With a fork, prick the potatoes.
2. Arrange potatoes into the greased air fryer basket.
3. Arrange the fryer basket in the center of Instant Omni Plus Toaster Oven.

4. Select "Air Fry" and then adjust the temperature to 355 degrees F.
5. Set the timer for 20 minutes and press "Start".
6. When the display shows "Turn Food" do nothing.
7. When cooking time is complete, remove from Toaster Oven and transfer the potatoes onto a platter.
8. In a bowl, add the remaining ingredients and mix until well combined.
9. Open potatoes from the center and stuff them with cheese mixture.
10. Serves immediately

STUFFED TOMATOES

Cooking Time: 15 minutes
Serves: 2

Ingredients
- 2 large tomatoes
- ½ cup broccoli, chopped finely
- ½ cup Cheddar cheese, shredded
- Salt and ground black pepper, as required
- 1 tablespoon unsalted butter, melted
- ½ teaspoon dried thyme, crushed

Directions
1. Carefully, cut the top of each tomato and scoop out pulp and seeds.
2. In a bowl, mix together chopped broccoli, cheese, salt and black pepper.
3. Stuff each tomato with broccoli mixture evenly.
4. Arrange the stuffed tomatoes into the greased air fryer basket.
5. Arrange the fryer basket in the center of Instant Omni Plus Toaster Oven.
6. Select "Air Fry" and then adjust the temperature to 355 degrees F.
7. Set the timer for 15 minutes and press "Start".
8. When the display shows "Turn Food" do nothing.
9. When cooking time is complete, remove the tomatoes from Toaster Oven.
10. Serves with the garnishing of thyme.

PARMESAN BROCCOLI

Cooking Time: 1520 minutes
Serves: 2

Ingredients
- 10 ounces frozen broccoli
- 3 tablespoons balsamic vinegar
- 1 tablespoon olive oil
- Salt and ground black pepper, as required
- 2 tablespoons Parmesan cheese, grated
- 1 teaspoon fresh lemon zest, grated

Directi o ns
1. In a bowl, add the broccoli, vinegar, oil, salt, and black pepper and toss to coat well.
2. Arrange the broccoli florets into the greased air fryer basket.
3. Arrange the fryer basket in the center of Instant Omni Plus Toaster Oven.
4. Select "Air Fry" and then adjust the temperature to 400 degrees F.
5. Set the timer for 15 minutes and press "Start".
6. When the display shows "Turn Food" flip the broccoli florets.
7. When cooking time is complete, remove the air fryer basket from Toaster Oven.
8. Transfer the broccoli onto serving plates.
9. Immediately, sprinkle with cheese and lemon zest and Serves hot.

GLAZED CARROTS

Cooking Time: 12 minutes
Serves: 4

Ingredients
- 3 cups carrots, peeled and cut into large chunks
- 1 tablespoon olive oil
- 1 tablespoon maple syrup

- 1 tablespoon fresh parsley, minced
- Salt and ground black pepper, as required

Directi o ns
1. In a bowl, add the carrot, oil, maple syrup, thyme, salt, and black pepper.
2. Arrange the carrot chunks into the greased air fryer basket in a single layer.
3. Arrange the fryer basket in the center of Instant Omni Plus Toaster Oven.
4. Select "Air Fry" and then adjust the temperature to 390 degrees F.
5. Set the timer for 12 minutes and press "Start".
6. When the display shows "Turn Food" flip the carrot chunks.
7. When cooking time is complete, remove the air fryer basket from Toaster Oven.
8. Serves hot.

BUTTERED ZUCCHINI

Cooking Time: 30 minutes
Serves: 6

Ingredients
- 2 tablespoons butter, melted and
- 2 pounds zucchinis, sliced
- 1 tablespoon fresh basil, chopped
- Salt and ground black pepper, as required

Directi o ns
1. In a bowl, mix together all the ingredients.
2. Arrange the zucchini slices into the greased air fryer basket in a single layer.
3. Arrange the fryer basket in the center of Instant Omni Plus Toaster Oven.
4. Select "Air Fry" and then adjust the temperature to 400 degrees F.
5. Set the timer for 30 minutes and press "Start".
6. When the display shows "Turn Food" flip the zucchini.
7. When cooking time is complete, remove the air fryer basket from Toaster Oven.
8. Serves hot.

SWEET & SPICY PARSNIPS

Cooking Time: 44 minutes
Serves: 5

Ingredients

- 1½ pounds parsnip, peeled and cut into 1-inch chunks
- 1 tablespoon butter, melted
- 2 tablespoons honey
- 1 tablespoon dried parsley flakes, crushed
- ¼ teaspoon red pepper flakes, crushed
- Salt and ground black pepper, as required

Directi o ns

1. In a large bowl, mix together the parsnips and butter.
2. Arrange the parsnip chunks into the greased air fryer basket in a single layer.
3. Arrange the fryer basket in the center of Instant Omni Plus Toaster Oven.
4. Select "Air Fry" and then adjust the temperature to 355 degrees F.
5. Set the timer for 44 minutes and press "Start".
6. Meanwhile, in another large bowl, mix together the remaining ingredients.
7. When the display shows "Turn Food" flip the parsnips chunks.
8. After 40 minutes of cooking, coat the parsnips chunks with honey mixture.
9. When cooking time is complete, remove the air fryer basket from Toaster Oven.
10. Serves hot.

TOFU IN ORANGE SAUCE

Cooking Time: 20 minutes
Serves: 4

Ingredients

For Tofu:

- 1 pound extra-firm tofu, pressed and cubed
- 1 tablespoon cornstarch
- 1 tablespoon low-sodium soy sauce

For Sauce:

- ½ cup water
- 1/3 cup fresh orange juice
- 1 tablespoon maple syrup
- 1 teaspoon orange zest, grated
- 1 teaspoon garlic, minced
- 1 teaspoon fresh ginger, minced
- 2 teaspoons cornstarch
- ¼ teaspoon red pepper flakes, crushed
- 2 scallions, chopped

Directions

1. In a bowl, add the tofu, cornstarch, and soy sauce and toss to coat well.
2. Set the tofu aside to marinate for at least 15 minutes.
3. Arrange the tofu cubes into the greased air fryer basket in a single layer.
4. Arrange the fryer basket in the center of Instant Omni Plus Toaster Oven.
5. Select "Air Fry" and then adjust the temperature to 390 degrees F.
6. Set the timer for 10 minutes and press "Start".
7. When the display shows "Turn Food" flip the tofu.
8. Meanwhile, for the sauce: in a small pan, add all the ingredients except for scallions over medium-high heat and bring to a boil, stirring continuously.
9. When cooking time is complete, remove the air fryer basket from Toaster Oven.
10. Transfer the tofu into a serving bowl
11. Top with the sauce and gently stir to combine.
12. Garnish with scallions and Serves.

SEAFOOD RECIPES

SALMON CROQUETTES

Cooking time: 10 minutes
Serves: 6-8

Ingredients
- Panko breadcrumbs
- Almond flour
- 2 egg whites
- 2 tbsp. Chopped chives
- 2 tbsp. Minced garlic cloves
- ½ c. Chopped onion
- 2/3 c. Grated carrots
- 1 pound (453.592g) chopped salmon fillet

Directions
1. Mix together all ingredients minus breadcrumbs, flour, and egg whites.
2. Shape mixture into balls. Then coat them in flour, then egg, and then breadcrumbs. Drizzle with olive oil.
3. Pour the coated salmon balls into the oven rack/basket. Place the rack on the middle-shelf of the air fryer oven. Set temperature to 350°f, and set time to 6 minutes. Shake and cook an additional 4 minutes until golden in color.

FRIED CALAMARI

Cooking time: 7 minutes
Serves: 6-8

Ingredients
- ½ tsp. Salt
- ½ tsp. Old bay seasoning
- 1/3 c. Plain cornmeal
- ½ c. Semolina flour
- ½ c. Almond flour
- 5-6 c. Olive oil
- 1 ½ pounds (680.389g) baby squid

Directi o ns
1. Rinse squid in cold water and slice tentacles, keeping just ¼-inch of the hood in one piece.
2. Combine 1-2 pinches of pepper, salt, old bay seasoning, cornmeal, and both flours together. Dredge squid pieces into flour mixture and place into the air fryer basket.
3. Spray liberally with olive oil. Cook 15 minutes at 345 degrees till coating turns a golden brown.

SOY AND GINGER SHRIMP

Cooking time: 10 minutes
Serves: 4

Ingredients
- 2 tablespoons olive oil
- 2 tablespoons scallions, finely chopped
- 2 cloves garlic, chopped
- 1 teaspoon fresh ginger, grated
- 1 tablespoon dry white wine
- 1 tablespoon balsamic vinegar
- 1/4 cup soy sauce
- 1 tablespoon sugar
- 1 pound (453.592g) shrimp
- Salt and ground black pepper, to taste

Directions
1. To make the marinade, warm the oil in a saucepan; cook all ingredients, except the shrimp, salt, and black pepper. Now, let it cool.
2. Marinate the shrimp, covered, at least an hour, in the refrigerator.
3. After that, pour into the oven rack/basket. Place the rack on the middle-shelf of the air fryer oven. Set temperature to 350°f, and set time to 10 minutes. Bake the shrimp at 350 degrees f for 8 to 10 minutes (depending on the size), turning once or twice. Season prepared shrimp with salt and black pepper and Serves.

PANKO-CRUSTED TILAPIA

Cooking time: 10 minutes
Serves: 3

INGREDIENTS
- 2 tsp. Italian seasoning
- 2 tsp. Lemon pepper
- 1/3 c. Panko breadcrumbs
- 1/3 c. Egg whites
- 1/3 c. Almond flour
- 3 tilapia fillets
- Olive oil

Directions
1. Place panko, egg whites, and flour into separate bowls. Mix lemon pepper and Italian seasoning in with breadcrumbs.
2. Pat tilapia fillets dry. Dredge in flour, then egg, then breadcrumb mixture.
3. Add to the air fryer basket and spray lightly with olive oil.
4. Cook 10-11 minutes at 400 degrees, making sure to flip halfway through cooking.

POTATO CRUSTED SALMON

Cooking time: 15 minutes
Serves: 4

Ingredients
- 1 pound (453.592g) salmon, swordfish or arctic char fillets, 3/4 inch thick
- 1 egg white
- 2 tablespoons water
- 1/3 cup dry instant mashed potatoes
- 2 teaspoons cornstarch
- 1 teaspoon paprika
- 1 teaspoon lemon pepper seasoning

Directi o ns
1. Remove and skin from the fish and cut it into 4 serving pieces mix together the egg white and water. Mix together all of the dry ingredients. Dip the filets into the egg white mixture then press into the potato mix to coat evenly.
2. Pour into the oven rack/basket. Place the rack on the middle-shelf of the air fryer oven. Set temperature to 360°f, and set time to 15 minutes, flip the filets halfway through.

SNAPPER SCAMPI

Cooking time: 10 minutes
Serves: 4

Ingredients
- 4 (6-ounce) skinless snapper or arctic char fillets
- 1 tablespoon olive oil
- 3 tablespoons lemon juice, divided
- ½ teaspoon dried basil
- Pinch salt
- Freshly ground black pepper
- 2 tablespoons butter
- Cloves garlic, minced

Directions
1. Rub the fish fillets with olive oil and 1 tablespoon of the lemon juice. Sprinkle with the basil, salt, and pepper, and place in the air fryer oven basket.
2. Grill the fish for 7 to 8 minutes or until the fish just flakes when tested with a fork. Remove the fish from the basket and put on a serving plate. Cover to keep warm. In a 6-by-6-by-2-inch pan, combine the butter, remaining 2 tablespoons lemon juice, and garlic. Cook in the air fryer oven for 1 to 2 minutes or until the garlic is sizzling. Pour this mixture over the fish and Serves.

THAI FISH CAKES WITH MANGO RELISH

Cooking time: 10 minutes
Serves: 4

Ingredients
- 1 lb. (453.592g) white fish fillets
- 3 tbsps. ground coconut
- 1 ripened mango
- ½ tsps. chili paste
- 2 Tbsps. fresh parsley
- 1 green onion
- 1 lime
- 1 tsp salt
- 1 egg

Directions

1. To make the relish, peel and dice the mango into cubes. Combine with a half teaspoon of chili paste, a tablespoon of parsley, and the zest and juice of half a lime.
2. In a food processor, pulse the fish until it forms a smooth texture. Place into a bowl and add the salt, egg, chopped green onion, parsley, two tablespoons of the coconut, and the remainder of the chili paste and lime zest and juice. Combine well
3. Portion the mixture into 10 equal balls and flatten them into small patties. Pour the reServesd tablespoon of coconut onto a dish and roll the patties over to coat.
4. Preheat the air fryer oven to 390 degrees
5. Place the fish cakes into the air fryer oven and cook for 8 minutes. They should be crisp and lightly browned when ready
6. Serves hot with mango relish

TUNA STUFFED POTATOES

Cooking time: 30 minutes
Serves: 4

Ingredients
- 4 starchy potatoes
- ½ tablespoon olive oil
- 1 (6-ounce) can tuna, drained
- 2 tablespoons plain Greek yogurt
- 1 teaspoon red chili powder
- Salt and freshly ground black pepper, to taste
- 1 scallion, chopped and divided
- 1 tablespoon capers

Directions
1. In a large bowl of water, soak the potatoes for about 30 minutes. Drain well and pat dry with paper towel.
2. Preheat the air fryer to 355 degrees f. Place the potatoes in a fryer basket.
3. Cook for about 30 minutes.
4. Meanwhile in a bowl, add tuna, yogurt, red chili powder, salt, black pepper and half of scallion and with a potato masher, mash the mixture completely.
5. Remove the potatoes from the air fryer oven and place onto a smooth surface.
6. Carefully, cut each potato from top side lengthwise.
7. With your fingers, press the open side of potato halves slightly. Stuff the potato open portion with tuna mixture evenly.
8. Sprinkle with the capers and remaining scallion. Serves immediately.

BAKED TILAPIA

Cooking Time: 15 minutes
Serves: 4

Ingredients
- 1 lb tilapia fillets
- 2 tbsp olive oil
- 2 tbsp dried parsley
- 2 tbsp garlic, minced
- Pepper
- Salt

Directions
1. Spray cooking pan with cooking spray and set aside.
2. Place fish fillets on cooking pan. Drizzle with oil and season with pepper and salt.
3. Sprinkle garlic and parsley over fish fillets.
4. Select bake mode and set the omni to 400 F for 15 minutes once the oven beeps, place the cooking pan into the oven.
5. Serves and enjoy.

LEMON PEPPER BASA

Cooking Time: 12 minutes
Serves: 4

Ingredients
- 4 basa fish fillets
- 1/4 tsp lemon pepper seasoning
- 4 tbsp fresh lemon juice
- 8 tsp olive oil
- 2 tbsp fresh parsley, chopped
- 1/4 cup green onion, sliced
- 1/4 tsp garlic powder
- Pepper
- Salt

Directions
1. Place fish fillets on cooking pan and spray with cooking spray.
2. Pour oil and lemon juice over fish fillets. Sprinkle remaining ingredients over fish fillets.
3. Select bake mode and set the omni to 425 F for 12 minutes once the oven beeps, place the cooking pan into the oven.
4. Serves and enjoy.

GINGER GARLIC FISH FILLETS

Cooking Time: 20 minutes
Serves: 2

Ingredients
- 12 oz swordfish fillets
- 1/8 tsp crushed red pepper
- 1 garlic clove, minced
- 2 tsp fresh parsley, chopped
- 3 tbsp olive oil
- 1/2 tsp lemon zest, grated
- 1/2 tsp ginger, grated

Directions
1. In a small bowl, mix together 2 tablespoon oil, lemon zest, red pepper, ginger, garlic, and parsley.
2. Season fish fillets with salt.
3. Heat remaining oil in a pan over medium-high heat.
4. Place fish fillets in the pan and cook until lightly browned 3 minutes.
5. Transfer fish fillets in a baking dish.
6. Select bake mode and set the omni to 400 F for 20 minutes once the oven beeps, place the baking dish into the oven.
7. Serves and enjoy.

CAJUN FISH FILLETS

Cooking Time: 15 minutes
Serves: 4

Ingredients
- 1 lb catfish fillets, cut ½-inch thick
- 2 tsp onion powder
- 1 tbsp dried oregano, crushed
- 1/2 tsp ground cumin
- 3/4 tsp chili powder
- 1 tsp crushed red pepper
- Pepper
- Salt

Directions
1. In a small bowl, mix together cumin, chili powder, crushed red pepper, onion powder, oregano, pepper, and salt.
2. Rub fish fillets with the spice mixture on both sides.
3. Place fish fillets in a baking dish.
4. Select bake mode and set the omni to 350 F for 15 minutes once the oven beeps, place the baking dish into the oven.
5. Serves and enjoy.

TASTY CAJUN SALMON

Cooking Time: 12 minutes
Serves: 2

Ingredients
- 1 lb salmon fillets
- 1/8 tsp cayenne pepper
- 1 tsp paprika
- 2 tsp onion powder
- 2 tsp garlic powder
- 2 tsp Cajun seasonings
- 3 tbsp olive oil
- 1/4 cup parsley, minced
- 1 lemon juice
- Pepper
- Salt

Directi o ns
1. In a small bowl, mix together Cajun seasoning, pepper, garlic powder, onion powder, paprika, cayenne pepper, and salt.
2. Brush fillets with oil and rub with spice mixture.
3. Place fish fillets in a baking dish. Pour lemon juice over fish fillets.
4. Select bake mode and set the omni to 450 F for 12 minutes once the oven beeps, place the baking dish into the oven.
5. Garnish with parsley and Serves.

EASY BAKED HALIBUT

Cooking Time: 15 minutes
Serves: 4

Ingredients
- 1 lb halibut fillets
- 1/4 tsp garlic powder
- 1/2 tsp paprika
- 1/4 cup olive oil
- Pepper
- Salt

Directions
1. Place fish fillets in a baking dish.
2. In a small bowl, mix together oil, garlic powder, paprika, pepper, and salt.
3. Brush fish fillets with oil mixture.
4. Select bake mode and set the omni to 425F for 15 minutes once the oven beeps, place the baking dish into the oven.
5. Serves and enjoy.

HONEY ORANGE SALMON

Cooking Time: 25 minutes

Serves: 8

Ingredients
- 1 lb salmon fillets
- 1 orange juice
- 1 orange zest, grated
- 2 tbsp honey
- 3 tbsp soy sauce

Directi o ns
1. In a small bowl, whisk together honey, soy sauce, orange juice, and orange zest.
2. Place salmon fillets in a baking dish and pour honey mixture over salmon fillets.
3. Select bake mode and set the omni to 425F for 7 minutes once the oven beeps, place the baking dish into the oven.
4. Flip salmon fillets and bake for 18 minutes more.
5. Serves and enjoy.

BLACKENED FISH FILLETS

Cooking Time: 12 minutes
Serves: 4

Ingredients
- 4 Mahi Mahi fillets
- 1/2 cayenne
- 1 tsp oregano
- 1 tsp cumin
- 1 tsp onion powder
- 1 tsp paprika
- 1 tsp garlic powder
- 3 tbsp Olive oil
- 1/2 tsp pepper
- 1/2 tsp salt

Directions
1. Line baking pan with parchment-lined paper and set aside.
2. Place fish fillets on the baking dish and drizzle with oil.
3. In a small bowl, mix together cumin, onion powder, paprika, cayenne, oregano, garlic powder, pepper, and salt.
4. Rub fish fillets with a spice mixture.
5. Select bake mode and set the omni to 450F for 12 minutes once the oven beeps, place the baking dish into the oven.
6. Serves and enjoy.

SNACKS & APPETIZERS RECIPES

CHICKEN SANDWICH

Cooking time: 15 minutes.
Serves: 2

Ingredients
- 2 cloves garlic
- Fresh parsley leaves
- 500g chopped breast
- 1 tsp Salt
- Pepper
- 1 egg L
- 50g milk
- 50g Cheese spread
- 14-16 slices sliced bread
- 7-8 slices semi-cured cheese

Directions
1. Chop the garlic and parsley.
2. Add the breast in pieces, salt, and pepper
3. Add the rest of the ingredients and spread slices!
4. Spread the paste on all the slices, cover half with a slice of cheese, and cover with another slice, cut into triangles and there are two options, pass them by egg and breadcrumbs
5. Preheat the 200C air fryer, about 8 or 10 minutes, until the bread becomes colored.

POTATO BALLS STUFFED WITH HAM AND CHEESE

Cooking time: 25 minutes.
Serves: 4

Ingredients
- 4 potatoes
- 100g cooked ham
- 100g of grated or grated cheese
- Salt
- Ground pepper
- Flour
- Oil

Directi o ns
1. Peel the potatoes and cut into quarters.
2. Put in a pot with water and bring to the fire, let cook until tender.
3. Drain and squeeze with a fork until the potatoes are made dough and season.
4. Add the ham and cheese.
5. Let's link everything.
6. Make balls and pass through the flour.
7. Spray with oil and go to the basket of the air fryer.
8. Select 20 minutes, 2000C for each batch of balls you put. Do not pile up because they would break down. From time to time remove from the basket so that they are made on all sides, you have to shake the basket so that the balls roll a little and Serves.

SPRING ROLLS

Cooking time: 30 minutes.
Serves: 6

Ingredients
- 8 sheets of Philo pasta
- 2 onions
- 2 carrots
- 1 piece of Chinese cabbage
- 75g of bean sprouts
- Salt
- Ground pepper
- Extra virgin olive oil
- 1 dash of soy sauce

Directions
1. Grate the carrots, cabbage, and onions.
2. Put in the Wok some extra virgin olive oil.
3. When it's hot, add the vegetables,
4. Season and sauté without losing the crunchy touch.
5. Incorporate the bean sprouts and the soy sauce.
6. Sauté and let temper so that the Philo pasta does not get very wet.
7. Extend the sheets, distribute the filling between the layers and roll up, in the form of a roll, that is, the filling in the center of the sheet. Give the first fold from the bottom up, then the sides mount them on top of each other, and now you end up spinning up its width.
8. Place in the basket of the air fryer, 2 in 2.
9. Paint with oil.
10. Select 20 minutes, 1800C.
11. Make all the rolls.
12. When you have them all done, place all in the basket of the air fryer, one over the other carefully. Select 5 minutes, 1800C, and give a heat stroke so that all are Servesd hot.

MINI BURGERS

Cooking time: 25 minutes.
Serves: 4

Ingredients
- 500g Minced pork
- Salt
- Ground pepper
- Garlic Powder
- Fresh parsley
- Spices
- 1 egg
- 1 tbsp grated bread
- Mini Bread for Burgers

Directions
1. Dress the meat of the hamburgers.
2. Add some salt to the ground beef, some ground pepper, garlic powder, a tablespoon of chopped fresh parsley, a teaspoon of spices.
3. Now, throw an egg and one or two teaspoons of breadcrumbs, so that the meat becomes more consistent. Stir all ingredients well until everything is integrated
4. Then, cover it with transparent and let it rest in the refrigerator for at least half an hour or more. It will be easier after handling the meat and giving it the shape of a hamburger.
5. Once the time has elapsed, take out the meat. Take it out of the paper that surrounds the container and begins to mold and make the mini burger.
6. To prepare them in the fryer:
7. First, heat the fryer. So, adjust the thermostat to 200ºC and the timer for about 5 minutes. When it is hot, the pilot or the green light will go out.
8. When half the time has passed, turn around so that they are done well by both parties.

SAUSAGES AND CHORIZOS

Cooking time: 20 minutes.

Serves: 2-4

Ingredients
- 300g of sausage or frozen sausages
- One tablespoon olive oil

Directi o ns
1. Remove sausages directly from the freezer and place them in the fryer basket.
2. To defrost sausages and remove some of their fat, you must boil them for 5 to 10 minutes, and then prick food to remove all the remaining fat.
3. Then separate the sausages and chorizos on a tray or bowl.
4. Add a tablespoon of your favorite oil (preferably olive oil) in the bowl and mix the sausage well with the oil.
5. Then place the sausages and chorizos in the fryer basket.
6. Program your fryer at a temperature of 190°C and the timer in about 10 minutes.
7. Then turn the sausage as well as chorizos and perform the same process with the fryer.
8. And finally, after 10 minutes, Serves and enjoy them.

SAUSAGE PUFF PASTRY

Cooking time: 20 minutes.
Serves: 1-4

Ingredients
- Amount needed of puff pastry
- Amount needed of sausages

Directi o ns
1. Cut the puff pastry into thin slices about 5 cm wide.
2. Divide the sausages into two pieces.
3. Preheat the air fryer a few minutes at 180oC.
4. Meanwhile, roll each piece of sausage with a strip of puff pastry and paint on top with beaten egg.
5. Place in the basket of the air fryer.
6. Set the timer 10 minutes at 180oC temperature.
7. Take as an appetizer at any time of the year. Kids love it.

FLANK STEAK WITH BALSAMIC MUSTARD

Cooking time: 2h 15 minutes.
Serves: 3

Ingredients
- 60 ml of olive oil
- 60 ml balsamic vinegar
- 36g Dijon mustard
- 16 oz flank steak
- Salt and pepper to taste
- 4 basil leaves, sliced

Directions
1. Mix olive oil, balsamic vinegar, and mustard. Mix them to create a marinade.
2. Put the steak directly in the marinade. Cover with plastic wrap and marinate in the fridge for 2 hours or at night.
3. Remove from the refrigerator and let it reach room temperature.
4. Preheat the air fryer by pressing Start/Pause.
5. Place the fillet in the preheated air fryer, select Fillet, and press Start/Pause.
6. Cut the steak at an angle through the muscle. Season with salt and pepper and decorate with the basil to Serves.

PINE SKEWERS ACETO REDUCTION

Cooking time: 15 minutes.
Serves: 2

Ingredients
- 1 small can of pineapple in its juice
- Necessary quantity Peeled prawns
- Skewers Sticks
- For the sauce:
- 150 ml of Balsamic Aceto
- 120g of sugar

Directions
1. Open a small can of pineapple in its juice and drain well.
2. Cut the pineapple slices into four parts and set aside.
3. Peel the prawns and take out the tail.
4. Preheat the air fryer at 180oC temperature for a few minutes and put the skewers in the basket. Program the timer about 10 minutes at 18000C.
5. To prepare the balsamic Aceto sauce: place the Aceto and sugar in a small pot. Reduce over low heat until it thickens but without letting caramel.
6. Let stand until it cools.

SPINACH CHIPS

Cooking Time: 10 minutes
Serves: 2

Ingredients
- 2 cups fresh baby spinach leaves
- 1 tablespoon canola oil
- Salt and ground black pepper, as required

Directions
1. In a bowl, add all the ingredients and toss to coat well.
2. Place the spinach leaves into the greased air fryer basket in a single layer.
3. Arrange the air fryer basket in the center of Instant Omni Plus Toaster Oven/
4. Select "Air Fry" and then adjust the temperature to 300 degrees F.
5. Set the timer for 10 minutes and press "Start".
6. When the display shows "Turn Food" do nothing.
7. When cooking time is complete, remove the air fryer basket from Toaster Oven.
8. Serves warm.

MOZZARELLA STICKS

Cooking Time: 12 minutes
Serves: 3

Ingredients
- 3 tablespoons all-purpose flour
- 2 eggs
- 3 tablespoons milk
- ½ cup breadcrumbs
- ½ pound mozzarella cheese block, cut into 3x½-inch sticks

Directions
1. In a shallow dish, place the flour.
2. In a second shallow dish, add the eggs and milk and beat well.
3. In a third shallow dish, place the breadcrumbs.
4. Coat the Mozzarella sticks with flour, then dip in egg mixture and finally, coat with the breadcrumbs.
5. Arrange the Mozzarella sticks onto a cookie sheet and freeze for about 1-2 hours.
6. Now, place the mozzarella sticks into the greased air fryer basket.
7. Arrange the air fryer basket in the center of Instant Omni Plus Toaster Oven.
8. Select "Air Fry" and then adjust the temperature to 400 degrees F.
9. Set the timer for 12 minutes and press "Start".
10. When the display shows "Turn Food" do nothing.
11. When cooking time is complete, remove the air fryer basket from Toaster Oven.
12. Serves warm.

AVOCADO FRIES

Cooking Time: 7 minutes
Serves: 4

Ingredients
- ¼ cup all-purpose flour
- Salt and ground black pepper, as required
- 1 egg
- 1 teaspoon water
- ½ cup seasoned breadcrumbs
- 1 avocado, peeled, pitted and sliced into 8 pieces
- Nonstick cooking spray

Directi o ns
1. In a shallow bowl, mix together the flour, salt, and black pepper.
2. In a second bowl, add the egg and water and beat well.
3. In a third bowl, place the breadcrumbs.
4. Coat the avocado slices with flour mixture, then dip into egg mixture and finally, coat evenly with the breadcrumbs.
5. Now, spray the avocado slices with cooking spray evenly.
6. Place the avocado slices into the greased air fryer basket.
7. Arrange the air fryer basket in the center of Instant Omni Plus Toaster Oven.
8. Select "Air Fry" and then adjust the temperature to 400 degrees F.
9. Set the timer for 7 minutes and press "Start".
10. When the display shows "Turn Food" do nothing.
11. When cooking time is complete, remove the air fryer basket from Toaster Oven.
12. Serves warm.

PANCETTA WRAPPED SHRIMP

Cooking Time: 7 minutes
Serves: 6

Ingredients
- 1 pound pancetta, thinly sliced
- 1 pound shrimp, peeled and deveined

Directions
1. Wrap each shrimp with one pancetta slice.
2. Arrange the shrimp in a baking dish and refrigerate for about 20 minutes.
3. Now, place the shrimp into the greased air fryer basket.
4. Arrange the air fryer basket in the center of Instant Omni Plus Toaster Oven.
5. Select "Air Fry" and then adjust the temperature to 390 degrees F.
6. Set the timer for 7 minutes and press "Start".
7. When the display shows "Turn Food" do nothing.
8. When cooking time is complete, remove the air fryer basket from Toaster Oven.
9. Serves warm.

SPICY CHICKEN WINGS

Cooking Time: 20 minutes
Serves: 4

Ingredients
- 1½ pounds chicken wing sections
- 1 tablespoon canola oil
- Salt and ground black pepper, as required
- ¼ cup hot wing sauce

Directions
1. In a bowl, add the chicken wings, oil, salt and black pepper and mix well.
2. Place the chicken wings into the greased air fryer basket in a single layer.
3. Arrange the air fryer basket in the center of Instant Omni Plus Toaster Oven.
4. Select "Air Fry" and then adjust the temperature to 400 degrees F.
5. Set the timer for 20 minutes and press "Start".
6. When the display shows "Turn Food" flip the wings.
7. When cooking time is complete, remove the air fryer basket from Toaster Oven.
8. Coat the chicken wings with wing sauce evenly.
9. Now, arrange the air fryer basket in the top of Instant Omni Plus Toaster Oven.
10. Select "Broil" and then set the timer for 1 minute.
11. Press "Start".
12. When cooking time is complete, remove the air fryer basket from Toaster Oven.
13. Serves warm.

HADDOCK NUGGETS

Cooking Time: 8 minutes
Serves: 5

Ingredients
- 1 cup all-purpose flour
- 2 eggs
- ¾ cup seasoned breadcrumbs
- 2 tablespoons vegetable oil
- 1 pound boneless haddock fillet, cut into strips

Directions
1. In a shallow dish, place the flour.
2. In a second dish, crack the eggs and beat well.
3. In a third dish, mix together the breadcrumbs and oil.
4. Coat the nuggets with flour, then dip into beaten eggs and finally, coat with the breadcrumbs.
5. Place the nuggets into the greased air fryer basket in a single layer.
6. Arrange the air fryer basket in the center of Instant Omni Plus Toaster Oven.
7. Select "Air Fry" and then adjust the temperature to 390 degrees F.
8. Set the timer for 8 minutes and press "Start".
9. When the display shows "Turn Food" flip the wings.
10. When cooking time is complete, remove the air fryer basket from Toaster Oven.
11. Serves warm.

PERFECT CRAB DIP

Cooking Time: 15 minutes
Serves: 8

Ingredients
- 1 cup cheddar cheese, shredded
- 8 oz lump crabmeat
- 2 green onion, sliced
- 1/2 tsp garlic powder
- 1 tsp old bay seasoning
- 1/4 cup mayonnaise
- 1/3 cup sour cream
- 8 oz cream cheese
- 1/2 tsp garlic salt

Directions
1. Add cream cheese, garlic powder, old bay seasoning, mayonnaise, sour cream, and garlic salt into the mixing bowl and beat until fluffy.
2. Add 1/2 cheddar cheese, crabmeat, and green onion and mix until just combined.
3. Pour cream cheese mixture into the 8*8-inch baking dish.
4. Select bake mode and set the omni to 375 F for 15 minutes once the oven beeps, place the baking dish into the oven.
5. Serves and enjoy.

SPICY ALMONDS

Cooking Time: 20 minutes
Serves: 6

Ingredients
- 1 1/2 cups raw almonds
- 1/2 tsp cayenne
- 1/4 tsp onion powder
- 1/4 tsp dried basil
- 1/2 tsp garlic powder
- 1/2 tsp cumin
- 1 1/2 tsp chili powder
- 2 tsp Worcestershire sauce
- 2 tbsp butter, melted
- 1/2 tsp sea salt

Directions
1. Line cooking pan with parchment paper and set aside.
2. In a mixing bowl, whisk together butter, Worcestershire sauce, chili powder, cumin, garlic powder, basil, onion powder, cayenne, and salt.
3. Add almonds and toss to coat.
4. Spread almonds onto the prepared cooking pan.
5. Select bake mode and set the omni to 350 F for 20 minutes once the oven beeps, place the cooking pan into the oven.
6. Serves and enjoy.

DESSERTS RECIPES

APPLE ROTATION

Cooking Time: 15 – 30 minutes
Serves: 6

Ingredients
- 1 roll of rectangular puff pastry
- 220g of apples
- 50g of sugar
- 100g raisins
- 50g pine nuts
- To taste breadcrumbs
- Cinnamon powder to taste

Directi o ns
1. Put the raisins in warm water for at least 30 min. Meanwhile, peel the apples, remove the kernel, and cut them into thin slices. Pour the apples into a large bowl and add the dried raisins.
2. Add the cinnamon, sugar, and pine nuts, gently mix the ingredients and let stand.
3. Meanwhile, spread the puff pastry on a work surface with parchment paper. Sprinkle with the breadcrumbs, leaving a 2-3 cm border around. Place the mixture in the center of the dough and close the coating along.
4. Be careful not to tear the dough, close the sides tightly so that the contents do not come out during cooking.
5. Place the liner on the air fryer and Cook over low temperature for about 25 min. When finished cooking, sprinkle the strudel with icing sugar and Serves warm sliced.

STUFFED BRIOCHE CROWN

Cooking Time: 30 – 45 minutes
Serves: 8

Ingredients
- 250g Manitoba flour
- 250g flour 00
- 200 ml of warm milk
- 100 ml of warm water
- 50 ml of olive oil
- 25g baker's yeast
- 1 tbsp sugar
- 1 tsp fine salt
- 250g cooked ham
- 8 slices of emmental cheese
- Poppy seeds
- 1 tbsp of water
- 1 tsp olive oil

Directi o ns
1. Prepare the brioche crown and let it grow in a lightly floured and closed container with food wrap for about an hour.
2. Once the survey is finished, spread the dough with a rolling pin, forming a narrow rectangle. First place the ham and then the cheese, leaving about 2 cm of free edge around.
3. Roll everything up to get a cylinder. Cut approximately 2 cm slices and place them in the basket covered with baking paper by placing them side by side to form a crown.
4. Let the preparation rise for another hour before cooking. In the end, brush with a mixture of warm water and oil over the entire surface of the crown and sprinkle with poppy seeds.
5. Preheat the air fryer at 180oC for 5 minutes. Cook for 40 minutes.

NUT CAKE

Cooking Time: 30-45 minutes
Serves: 10

Ingredients
- 250 g of walnuts
- 150g Maïzena
- 4 medium eggs
- 200g of butter (room temperature)
- 1 sachet of yeast
- 1 sachet of vanilla sugar
- 200g of sugar

Directi o ns
1. Chop the nuts with 50 g of sugar. Using a food processor, beat the butter with the remaining sugar until you get a shiny and foamy mixture.
2. Add the eggs one by one, making sure the mixture is still soft, then add the vanilla.
3. Add the chopped nuts with the sugar and then the cornstarch that will sift with the yeast.
4. Butter and flour the basket, then pour the mixture in the center.
5. Set the air fryer at 180oC.
6. Cook for 45 minutes (turn off the lower heating element 40 minutes later). Let cool before serving.

GENOISE CAKE

Cooking Time: 30-45 minutes
Serves: 10

Ingredients
- 6 eggs
- 190g of sugar
- 150g of flour 00 (flour 55)
- 75g potato starch
- 2g vanilla sugar

Directi o ns
1. In a bowl, beat the eggs with the sugar until you get a light and smooth mixture. Add the sifted flour, starch and vanilla sugar and mix with a whisk until a homogeneous mixture is obtained.
2. Butter and flour the basket, then pour the mixture.
3. Set the air fryer to 180oC and simmer for 35 minutes.

FROZEN SORRENTINO GNOCCHI

Cooking Time: 0 – 15 minutes
Serves: 2

Ingredients
- 550 g Sorrentino gnocchi

Directi o ns
1. Pour the gnocchi in the basket and cook for 13 minutes at 150OC mixing once halfway through cooking.

KHACHAPURI (GEORGIAN BREAD)

Cooking Time: 15 – 30 minutes
Serves: 4

Ingredients
- 500g of flour
- 450g whole yogurt
- ½ tsp baking soda
- ½ tsp salt
- 150 g ricotta
- 100g provokes smoked
- 150g Greek feta cheese
- 4 tbsp fine parsley

Directi o ns
1. Prepare the khachapuri dough by mixing all the ingredients until a smooth and homogeneous mixture is obtained. Divide the dough into 8 equal parts.
2. Form 8 balls cover them with a clean cloth. Let them rest in a warm place and away from drafts. After about 1 hour of lifting, start spreading the dough.
3. Meanwhile, prepare the filling by grating provokes smoked and the feta cheese and then mix with the ricotta and parsley.
4. Spread the 8 balls by hand in circles of 10 to 15 cm, fill 4 circles with the previously prepared filling and close with the other 4. Now roll the 4 khachapuri with a roller until you get a diameter of the size of the basket.
5. Grease the bottom of the basket and place 1 khachapuri. Also grease the surface and prick with a fork.
6. Set the air fryer to 180OC and cook each khachapuri for 15 minutes.

MARBLE CAKE

Cooking Time: 45-60 minutes
Serves: 10

Ingredients
- 190g Butter
- 1g bag of vanilla sugar
- 12g baking powder
- 375g Flour
- 22g cocoa powder
- 4g medium eggs
- 225g of sugar
- 165 ml of milk
- Salt (a pinch)

Directions
1. Put the previously softened butter into small pieces in a bowl with the sugar, mount the ingredients until a white and foamy cream forms.
2. Add the eggs at room temperature, one by one, the salt and beat about 5 minutes until you get a mixture without lumps. Add the flour (except 30 g that will keep aside), the yeast and vanilla sugar sifted alternately with the milk.
3. Mix the ingredients well, then divide them evenly and add the remaining flour in a bowl and the sifted cocoa in another.
4. Butter and flour the basket and first place the transparent mixture divided into three separate parts. Do the same with the dark mixture by filling the remaining gaps between the light mixture.
5. To get the veined effect, rotate a fork from top to bottom through the two colors of the mixture.
6. Set the air fryer to 1800C and cook for 40 minutes and then turn off the lower resistance.
7. Cook for another 10 min. Control the baking of the cake with the tip of a knife.

APPLE, CREAM, AND HAZELNUT CRUMBLE

Cooking Time: 15-30 minutes
Serves: 6

Ingredients
- 4 golden apples
- 100 ml of water
- 50g cane sugar
- 50g of sugar
- ½ tbsp cinnamon
- 200 ml of fresh cream
- Chopped hazelnuts to taste

Directions
1. In a bowl, combine the peeled apples, cut into small cubes, cane sugar, sugar, and cinnamon.
2. Pour the apples inside the basket, add the water. Set the air fryer to 180oC and simmer for 15 minutes depending on the type of apple used and the size of the pieces.
3. At the end, divide the apples in the serving glasses, cover with previously whipped cream and sprinkle with chopped hazelnuts.

BANANA MUFFINS

Cooking Time: 25 minutes
Serves: 12

Ingredients
- 1 2/3 cups all-purpose flour
- 1 teaspoon baking soda
- 1 teaspoon baking powder
- ½ teaspoon ground cinnamon
- ¼ teaspoon ground nutmeg
- ¼ teaspoon ground ginger
- ½ teaspoon salt
- 4 ripe bananas, peeled and mashed
- 2 eggs
- ½ cup brown sugar
- 1 teaspoon vanilla extract
- 3 tablespoon milk
- 1 tablespoon Nutella
- ¼ cup almonds, chopped

Directions
1. In a large bowl, sift together the flour, baking soda, baking powder, spices and salt.
2. In another bowl, mix together the remaining ingredients except walnuts.
3. Add the banana mixture into flour mixture and mix until just combined.
4. Fold in the almonds.
5. Place the mixture into 12 greased muffin molds evenly.
6. Arrange a sheet pan in the center of Instant Omni Plus Toaster Oven.
7. Place the muffin molds over the sheet pan.
8. Select "Air Fry" and then adjust the temperature to 248 degrees F.
9. Set the timer for 25 minutes and press "Start".
10. When the display shows "Turn Food" do nothing.
11. When cooking time is complete, remove the muffin molds from Toaster Oven and place the pan onto a wire rack for about 10 minutes.
12. Carefully, invert the muffins onto the wire rack to completely cool before serving.

CHOCOLATE MUFFINS

Cooking Time: 10 minutes
Serves: 9

Ingredients
- 1½ cups all-purpose flour
- ¼ cup sugar
- 2 teaspoons baking powder
- ½ teaspoon salt
- 1 cup plain Greek yogurt
- 1/3 cup olive oil
- 1 egg
- 1½ teaspoons vanilla extract
- ¼ cup semi-sweet mini chocolate chips
- ¼ cup walnuts, chopped

Directi o ns
1. In a bowl, mix well flour, sugar, baking powder, and salt.
2. In another bowl, add the yogurt, oil, egg, and vanilla extract and whisk until well combined.
3. Add the flour mixture and mix until just combined.
4. Fold in the chocolate chips and walnuts.
5. Place the mixture into 9 greased muffin molds evenly.
6. Arrange a sheet pan in the center of Instant Omni Plus Toaster Oven.
7. Place the muffin molds over the sheet pan.
8. Select "Air Fry" and then adjust the temperature to 355 degrees F.
9. Set the timer for 10 minutes and press "Start".
10. When the display shows "Turn Food" do nothing.
11. When cooking time is complete, remove the muffin molds from Toaster Oven and place the pan onto a wire rack for about 10 minutes.
12. Carefully, invert the muffins onto the wire rack to completely cool before serving.

WHITE CHOCOLATE CHEESECAKE

Cooking Time: 34 minutes
Serves: 6

Ingredients
- 3 eggs (whites and yolks separated)
- 1 cup white chocolate, chopped
- ½ cup cream cheese, softened
- 2 tablespoons unsweetened cocoa powder
- 2 tablespoons powdered sugar
- ¼ cup raspberry jam

Directions
1. In a bowl, add the egg whites and refrigerate to chill before using.
2. In a microwave-safe bowl, add the chocolate and microwave on high heat for about 2 minutes, stirring after every 30 seconds.
3. In the bowl of chocolate, add the cream cheese and microwave for about 1-2 minutes or until cream cheese melts completely.
4. Remove from microwave and stir in cocoa powder and egg yolks.
5. Remove the egg whites from refrigerator and whisk until firm peaks form.
6. Add 1/3 of the mixed egg whites into cheese mixture and gently, stir to combine.
7. Fold in the remaining egg whites.
8. Place the mixture into a 6-inch cake pan.
9. Arrange a sheet pan in the center of Instant Omni Plus Toaster Oven.
10. Place the cake pan over the sheet pan.
11. Select "Air Fry" and then adjust the temperature to 285 degrees F.
12. Set the timer for 30 minutes and press "Start".
13. When the display shows "Turn Food" do nothing.
14. When cooking time is complete, remove the muffin molds from Toaster Oven and place the pan onto a wire rack to cool completely.
15. Then, refrigerate to chill before serving.
16. Just before serving, dust with the powdered sugar.
17. Spread the jam evenly on top and Serves.

www.ingramcontent.com/pod-product-compliance
Lightning Source LLC
Chambersburg PA
CBHW081120080526
44587CB00021B/3677